LEOPARDS

LEOPARDS

FRITZ PÖLKING

Evans Mitchell Books

Contents

Introduction

Cats are among the most fascinating creatures on earth, and the leopard is perhaps the "ultimate" cat. We humans find their behaviour and their powerful, elegant movements quite thrilling. When you get to see these beautiful creatures up close, you can almost lose yourself in their alert and inquisitive gaze.

Encounters with this spotted member of the cat family are highlights of any Africa visit – unfortunately, such encounters occur all too rarely, all too briefly, and often during twilight. Furthermore, they almost always happen by chance, because leopards often wander for up to 5 km during the night: the last place you will find them the next morning is the place where you left them the previous evening.

In the Masai Mara in Kenya, I had the good fortune of being able to follow a family of leopards with my camera over a period of many years – even if I often only got to see them once every 14 days.

If you want to see a leopard in the wild, then you will spend 96% of your time looking for one and only 5% actually watching it. Leopards have a 'home range' of perhaps 40 square kilometres, within which there are hundreds of nooks and crannies where you will never ever find them. So you must simply drive around their territory day after day, hoping that after 3, 6 or 14 days a leopard will be kind enough to leave a gazelle in a tree, where you can then – perhaps – find it and watch it.

Left: As long as the cubs are still small and cannot go hunting with their mother, she prefers to bring small pieces of prey back to the cave, as these will not drag along the ground and leave trails for hyenas and lions to latch on to.

Above: In the very first weeks, the female leopard prefers to stay in the cave with her cubs the whole day long, only peeping out occasionally and leaving them only briefly to go to the toilet.

The most 'auspicious' time for a leopard-watcher or leopard photographer are the few weeks in the year when the female leopard (or lcopardess) hides her young in a cave or other hiding place, and when the cubs are between two and four months old. During this time the little ones are still rather static. Their mother often comes by with small bits of prey, or leaves the cave for a time, and you will have a good chance of catching sight of either her or her cubs. There is also a good chance that the mother will still be there in the morning, or that she will return in the evening shortly before darkness falls.

History and Distribution

The leopard had, and has, the widest distribution of all the big cats. Up until around 1.5 million years ago, leopards existed not only in Africa and Asia, but also in Europe – even as far as England.

The classification of this cat according to the zoological system undertaken by Carl von Linne is still valid today. Accordingly, the leopard belongs to the order Carnivora (carnivores), the family Felidae (cats), the genus Panthera (big cats), and has the species name Leopard or Panther (Panthera pardus). The leopard is extremely adaptable. According to Latham's observations from 1926, he found a petrified leopard cadaver at a height of 5642 m up Mount Kilimanjaro.

According to Guggisberg's account of 1966-1968, climbers on Mawenzie in the Kilimanjaro region heard the sounds of leopards at a height of 4209 m, and actually found some on Kibo at a height of 4575 m.

Left: A famous leopard region in the Masai Mara, with the Leopard Canyon in the foreground.

When pressure is exerted on cat populations in an area due to human habitation, the Cheetahs are the first to leave, followed by the lions, and lastly by the leopards. There are many stories of leopards remaining hidden right in the middle of a village during the day, only to disappear during the following night.

Leopard distribution in Africa*

Above: An ideal leopard 'biotope': rocks; high, easy-to-climb trees; long grass.

Opposite, top: A leopard is often almost invisible because of its camouflaged coat.

African Leopard.
Panthera pardus pardus

Sinai Leopard.
Panthera pardus jarvis

Barbary Leopard.
Panthera pardus panthera

Zanzibar Leopard.
Panthera pardus adersi

Disribution of leopards across the world, by seven sub-species[*]

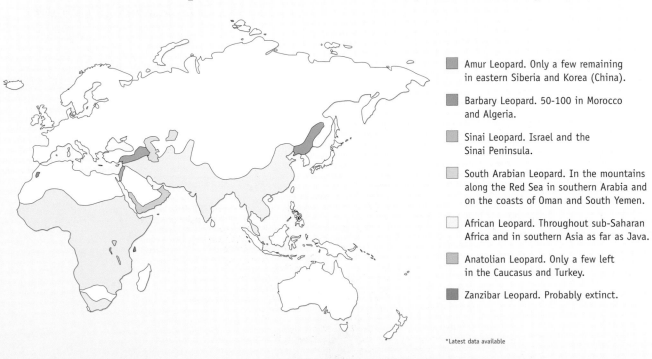

Amur Leopard. Only a few remaining in eastern Siberia and Korea (China).

Barbary Leopard. 50-100 in Morocco and Algeria.

Sinai Leopard. Israel and the Sinai Peninsula.

South Arabian Leopard. In the mountains along the Red Sea in southern Arabia and on the coasts of Oman and South Yemen.

African Leopard. Throughout sub-Saharan Africa and in southern Asia as far as Java.

Anatolian Leopard. Only a few left in the Caucasus and Turkey.

Zanzibar Leopard. Probably extinct.

*Latest data available

Distinguishing Features

Because of the variety of habitats in which leopards are found, and the different climatic conditions in which they exist, a great variety has developed in terms of behaviour and physical appearance. Its spotted coat (though the spots are actually rosettes) is ideally suited to making the leopard almost invisible in its native territory, and for serving as camouflage. These markings on the coat differ for each individual animal, and you can practically recognise each individual leopard by the markings on its face.

At high altitudes and in the rainforests, the coat tends towards being black all over, and here the leopard is often known as the 'black panther'. Its teeth are like daggers, and its canines are wonderful for holding onto prey and delivering the killer bite.

Leopards have thick cushioning under their teeth. They tread softly, with their weight borne on their toes (so-called 'digitigrades'), which is also very important because leopards cannot outrun their prey in the way that cheetahs can, and must creep up on them instead.

Left: The leopard is a remarkable cat. Here, it has caught a zebra during the night and carried it into a tree. To grip prey of this weight tight in its teeth and to carry it up a smooth tree trunk really is a breathtaking feat.

Above: Here the leopard has come upon a mother impala and its fawn, and is now creeping up on them, always keeping the prey fixed in its sights.

Leopards have excellent hearing, and the long hairs on their heads are not there just to impress us humans, but are also very useful for "sizing up" the dense thickets which surround them in their habitats.

Leopard males are around 60-70 cm long and weigh 35-65 kg. Females measure around 57-64 cm and weigh 28-58 kg, that is, they are generally smaller and lighter.

Leopards are both loners and generalists. They live in forests, savannahs, in the bush, in mountains, in deserts and in grassland. They eat virtually everything, from insects to white-bearded gnu.

Compared to bears, leopards are much more expressive, and you can always tell exactly how a leopard is feeling just by looking at it. Whether it is angry or content, whether it feels at ease or is irritated, it has a broad and multi-faceted mode of expression.

When a leopard lies dozing in a tree, its face is relaxed. But if its cubs start pestering it for something – be it milk or to play a game – and it doesn't want to be disturbed, then its facial expression becomes decidedly angry. The leopard's walk is a so-called "trot", and it usually saunters across its territory in a very relaxed manner, with its tail held slightly upwards. But when the leopard approaches its prey, it becomes completely flat, and moves slowly and very low over the ground.

Opposite page, top left: As we know from our pet cats, the leopard is a very clean animal and spends a lot of time grooming. Its tongue comes in very handy for this.

Opposite page, top right: A mother leopard is angry, because her 12-month old daughter wants to come close to her. Mummy is clearly not pleased!

Previous pages: Here a leopard first climbs up the trunk and then comes back down again. It is interesting to see the different techniques used when climbing up and down.

Habitat and Diet

Given the choice, leopards prefer to live in heavily-featured areas of land with lots of ditches, rocky caves, hiding places, undergrowth, and high trees which stand slightly diagonally to the ground, making them easier to climb. If there are also a large number of young, innocent, easily-captured animals around, then the leopard is happy. On top of that, if there are no humans, hyenas or lions then the leopard is in paradise, and could happily live in such a place for a thousand years or more!

Food and shelter – that is really almost everything that a leopard needs. In east Africa, their preference is for Thompson gazelles and impalas, but they also eat hares, zebras, young white-bearded gnus and virtually any kind of small animal that they can catch.

They are of course carnivores, which you can tell just by looking at their teeth. In the Londolozi Game Reserve in South Africa, the leopard is known to prey on 23 different types of animal. In the Krüger National Park the number is 21.

Opposite page: On the previous day, a strong male leopard caught a white-bearded gnu and left it lying under the tree, because it was too heavy to carry. He then ate as much of it has he could under the tree trunk, so as to then be able to carry the remaining, lighter portion onto this comfortable branch.

This page: A young, twelve-month old leopardess had caught her first impala, but wasn't able to carry it safely into the tree. But the following morning the prey was somehow in the tree! During the night, the mother leopard had helped her daughter to carry the animal into its branches.

When leopards hunt, you don't get the impression that they are after any particular animal or any particular species, except if there is a little cub waiting in a cave to be fed. Then leopards will go rummaging around the territory for hares, because they can easily be carried over long distances back to their young, and because they do not leave drag trails behind them as larger animals do. These tracks can then tempt lions and hyenas to follow the trail back to the leopard cubs.

The ability to creep up on prey is the hunting technique favoured by leopards. They try to come as close as possible to the prey, so that they can take them by surprise and capture the animal before it has any chance to run. Sometimes leopards do prefer to lie in wait, though, waiting in trees to jump down upon their prey.

Left: Carrying dinner: this leopardess was lying under a bush 30 m to the right of my car, playing with her daughter. Suddenly, 50m to the left of my car, a mother impala appeared on top of the hill with her fawn. The leopardess slid under my car, ran at the impalas and caught the fawn. Here we see her bringing the fawn to her daughter. This time, she doesn't crawl under my car, but crosses the open ground in front of it.

Above: Here, the leopard has caught a Thompson gazelle, who was grazing all alone in a landscape dense with bushes and trees, with few pairs of eyes to keep a lookout. That was a fatal error.

Leopards can only hunt relatively slow and inexperienced prey in the typical cheetah-like manner. Only very seldom do leopards pursue their prey over distances of 50 – 100 m and then catch them. After a successful hunt in areas where there are many hyenas and lions, leopards nearly always try to carry their prey into high trees for safety. Sometimes they only manage to do this at the very last minute, and I have often seen leopards carrying their dinner to safety just seconds ahead of the competition.

Where there are no competitors for their food, they often prefer to leave it lying on the ground. Sometimes, though, the food is very heavy and so the leopard will eat at it until it is light enough to carry. Or the leopard may drag it to another tree which is easier to climb.

Left: Here, the leopard has caught a baby gnu and has had to run quickly into a tree with it, because the furious mother gnu was chasing him.

Above: Early one morning I met this leopard with its breakfast. Blue eggs make a nice change!

33

Social Structure and Communication

There are still leopards to be found throughout Africa, wherever they can hunt prey and where humans let them, in forests, savannahs, in the bush and in the mountains, in grassland and even in deserts. Because leopards prefer the twilight and the night time, you don't see them as often as you see day-time cats. Added to which, leopards love shelter and they are very seldom to be found lying on a termite mound – one of the cheetah's favourite places and one where they can often and easily be found.

Because leopards like to live furtively, you hardly ever hear them either. The female may call out during the night during the mating season, or when she returns to talk to her cubs, but apart from that the leopard is virtually silent. Although they live alone in their territories of many square kilometres (the size of the territory depending on the landscape, food and competition), one morning I counted nine leopards in the Nairobi National Park in a territory of 20 km2, among them a mother with four cubs of nearly one year old.

When fellow members of the species meet one another "by accident", then threatening behaviour often ensues, with the appropriate facial expressions and noises. You'll hear hissing and snarling, and serious fights are not uncommon. Thus a report by the Kenya Game Department reports that a leopardess was once found killed by a blow to the skull, inflicted by a male leopard, and a female leopard was killed by a male in a fight over a dead impala.

Leopards have a 'living zone' and a 'prowling zone'. The living zone is marked off and defended against other leopards, whereby the incumbent usually wins any battles due to "home advantage". The prowling zone is not – or is much less often – marked, but it is not defended. The prowling zone will probably include the edges of other (female) living zones, whereby a male territory is significantly larger, overlapping with perhaps three female territories. This guarantees the male leopard access to several different females. These territorial markings are made using sounds, scratch marks on trees or on the ground, but mainly by use of smell.

Left: One of my most "sensational" leopard pictures. A situation such as this has perhaps never before been photographed, or even thought possible. Here, a mother leopard is lying in front of the cave watching over her two small cubs, about two months old, who are making their first attempts at play in front of the cave. Above them on a rock lies the leopard's other, twelve-month-old daughter, attentively watching her mother and her two little siblings.

Above: The twelve-month-old daughter is playing with her mother's little cubs, which the mother allows from time to time, but not always. This, too, has probably never been photographed before. Both of these pictures were taken in an area of the Masai Mara known as 'Figtree Avenue'.

Opposite page: Here, a leopard has left his captured prey in a tree and then forgotten about it! The leopard did not return, and the dried-out skeleton was still hanging in the tree a full year later.

This page: The leopard ran into a tree carrying a hare, chased by a hyena. Except where food is concerned, relations between leopards and hyenas are usually quite relaxed.

Reproduction and Growing Up

Normally, female leopards can give birth every two years. Between one and four cubs are born at intervals of around 25 months, following a gestation period of 90-100 days. Sometimes it happens earlier though. I knew a leopardess in the Masai Mara who brought twins into the world almost exactly twelve months after the birth of two cubs.

Of course, baby leopards only happen if the female leopard has been ready to mate. This receptiveness only lasts for around 6-7 days in every month, and repeats every month until she becomes pregnant. In order to become pregnant, the leopardess prowls around those areas which overlap with male territories, bellowing in a way which you would otherwise never hear at this volume.

The female leopard can give birth to up to four cubs, but usually no more than one or two of them survive the first weeks. This also depends on how experienced a mother she is and how many dangerous situations she can avoid or prevent. If there are few lions and hyenas in the area then this is of course very beneficial for the successful rearing of the cubs.

Left: A rare sight: The female leopard allows a very small cub to lie beside her in front of the cave.

Above: When the cubs are very small, the female leopard often stays in the cave the whole day long. For two weeks, this mother leopard only came out between 10 and 11 in the morning to go to the toilet, and disappeared back into the cave after about ten minutes to be with the two youngsters.

Opposite page, top left: When the mother leaves the little ones home alone during the day, you will hardly ever see them. Only very occasionally do they dare to leave the cave on their own.

Opposite page top right: The female leopard allows very small cubs to remain outside the cave for only a very short space of time, before she quickly pulls them back in to safety.

Opposite page bottom: At aged two months, the cubs can already follow their mother from one hiding place to another by themselves, and no longer need to be carried.

Right: Here, the female leopard is bringing a live hare back for her cubs so that they can gain experience. You can see this in the way she is carrying it. One sees this kind of behaviour much more often in the case of cheetahs. It is more difficult to observe in leopards, because of their secretive lifestyle.

Below: Here, a leopard's twelve-month-old daughter of is playing with one of her mother's small cubs of around two months old. A leopardess allowing her older cubs to play with the "new" generation has hardly ever been photographed before.

The bond between the cubs and their mother is strong, and I have myself seen how the mother leopard develops a particularly strong connection and affection if she only has one cub. In such cases she will often spend much more time and pay much more attention to the only cub.

But here, too, it is clear that the leopard is a loner. I have often been able to observe a female leopard leaving her two small cubs in the morning, one or two hours after sunrise, to rest in a hollow or on a high branch one or two kilometres away, which is actually rather a pointless exercise when you think about it.

She was always just far enough away that she could no longer hear or see any sign of her cubs. If they had been put in danger by lions or hyenas, she would of course have been unable to do anything at all to help them.

Opposite page, top: This little leopard is playing on a tree trunk while its mother lies a few metres away in the grass.

Opposite page, bottom: You hardly ever see leopards this small – they are usually kept well hidden by their mothers. In these first few weeks of life, the leopard still has blue eyes, as you can clearly see in this photo, which become yellow as they grow older.

Above: At the age of three months, the cubs are now bold enough to frolic around and play during the day, even when their mother is away.

Previous double page: Drinking, playing and training for adult life.

Left: Young leopards seem to love hitting their mother with their paws for fun.

Above: Here, the mother leopard is drinking with one of her cubs.

In the first few weeks, the female leopard frequently moves from one hiding place to another, sometimes each night, sometimes every week. But I have also seen a leopardess who stayed for six weeks at a time in the same, 1 km2 spot with her three-month-old daughter. Whether they move around because of inner insecurity, or because they recognise a real danger, is difficult for us humans to say.

Usually the female leopard leaves her cubs alone during the day and returns in the evening just before twilight, to be greeted excitedly by her little ones. Often she will play with the cubs for a while before lying on her side so that the cubs can drink milk from her. From what I have observed, the cubs begin to eat meat at aged 2-3 months. By this time they are also able to follow behind their mother as she moves from one hiding place to another.

A baby leopard which weighs about 400-500 grams at birth, will already weigh 3 kg by the time it is three months old, and after six months approximately 10 kg.

The leopard cubs love to play with their mother, and the games often end with the leopards grooming one another.

Right: This little leopard was on its way somewhere with its mother when two hyenas suddenly appeared. It immediately ran into this tree, where it began to shout insults at the hyenas, while its sister huddled close to their mother while the two of them lay on the ground, waiting for the hyenas to retreat.

Left and below: A dramatic situation. Baboons had discovered the caves where the baby leopards were hidden and then began to beset the mother, who was lying in front of the cave to protect her cubs. To start with, she hissed at the baboons, before displaying quite extraordinary behaviour: She lay on her side and just stared at the baboons, who never really had the stomach for a full-scale attack. After about 10-15 minutes they retreated.

At aged 18 months, young leopards often kill their first large animal, and begin to leave their mother. But in the Masai Mara I have seen leopards as young as 12 months old kill their first impala and become independent. However, the weaning process is probably much slower and more subtle than we have previously imagined, because leopards live so furtively, and at times in history have been so shy, such as when they were being hunted all over Africa, that observations of social behaviour were practically impossible.

Left: A leopardess with two young cubs around 6 months old in a tree. She slowly grows impatient due to the proximity of the cubs who are pestering her, as you can clearly see from her facial expression.

Above: A tragic moment. During the night, a lioness has killed this female leopard's daughter as she was crossing a clearing with her daughter and son. The daughter was exactly one year old. In the morning the mother leopard sat on a nearby branch until approximately 11 o'clock, before coming and sitting next to her dead daughter, to say goodbye. After five minutes she stood up, walked slowly away, and never returned.

Whereas today you are almost guaranteed to see leopards at least once or twice during a two-week stay in one of Kenya or Tanzania's national parks, 30 years ago you could have made umpteen visits of several weeks' duration without seeing hide nor hair of one.

Today, we are in a much better position to observe the behaviour of leopards, and we discover that the mother/cub relationship lasts for many years, and perhaps never actually ends at all.

Even if the cubs become independent after 12-24 months, you can sometimes still see certain leopard mothers and daughters munching on the same animal even years later, and I often got the impression that an adult daughter was leaving food in such a way that her mother and her new cubs could eat from it. In other words, the daughter was in some way helping to "bring up" her younger brothers and sisters.

Right: What's going on between mother and daughter in this picture only the camera can capture. Only wildlife photography can give us such pure slices of life, and make them visible. No glance and no thought is fast enough to capture it. Only the camera can do it. What each of the two cats is doing, and what they mean by their behaviour, can be gloriously seen in this photograph. For the daughter is not attacking her mother at all. Although she is apparently attacking with jowls open, with threatening fangs and bristling whiskers, at the same time her ears are demonstrating total submission, and thus giving the game away that her attack is a pretence. The mother leopard knows this of course, which can be seen from the fact that her ears are set at a friendly angle and her moustache is "at ease". And her look says it all: Child – must you really act so wild?

FROM REAL LIFE:

From a Mother and her Young Cubs

I first saw the leopardess called "Paradise" in December 1991. I was parked in a Toyota Landcruiser in Kenya's Masai Mara Game Reserve, next to a ditch near "Fig-Tree Avenue", watching a cheetah who was resting in the ditch with her five cubs and giving the impression that she was asleep.

Suddenly she shot up and disappeared over to the other side of me, in the ditch behind a bend. Thirty metres further on, two cats appeared out of the ditch in a wild chase – first a leopard, and then the cheetah which was chasing it and trying to drive it away. Around two hundred metres further on, both of them stopped and started growling at one another from a distance. By chance, five Land Rovers full of tourists from Governor's Camp arrived at that moment and parked in between the two cats, thereby breaking the eye contact between them. A little later the cheetah went back to her cubs and the leopard went in the other direction, towards Fig-Tree Avenue.

Left: My first meeting with Half-Tail. As you can see, in this picture she is still Long-Tail! In the background you can see the cheetah, which was probably killed by Half-Tail a few days later.

The leopardess was not at all shy of the cars all around her. Or to be more precise, she paid the vehicles no attention and treated them as if they were not there. Here I was able to capture my first portrait of this very special leopard. At that time of course I had no inkling of the things we would come to experience together. And of course I did not know her name. I only came to know all of this later, when I compared the photos of this meeting with photographs from later on. Because, just as each human being can be identified by their fingerprints, each leopard can be identified by the markings on their coat. It is in fact a leopard "fingerprint".

Three days after this meeting, the cheetah and her five cubs were killed by a leopard. The leopard was probably Paradise, the "owner" of the territory around Fig-Tree Avenue and Leopard Canyon. The camp drivers in the northern Masai Mara had given this young leopardess the name "Paradise", because shortly beforehand she had come from the Paradise Plain in the Masai Mara Game Reserve to this territory beyond limits of the game reserve, and had made it her home.

She was born on the Paradise Plain in August 1987, and lived there with her mother until 1989, before she found her independence in this region beyond the reserve, arriving here at the end of 1989. Fig-Tree Avenue and Leopard Canyon – situated on Masai Grassland – are an ideal leopard 'biotope', with rocks, beautiful and comfortable (for leopards!) fig trees, ditches ideal for creeping along in, very few lions and hyenas, but a large quantity of suitable prey.

Above and opposite page: Half-Tail, completely relaxed in the here-and-now.

PARADISE AND HER MOTHER

Her mother was a large, almost giant leopard, who was very shy – unlike her daughter. Her home was a territory near the Kiboko Crossing on the Paradise Plain. She could still be seen there up until about 1993. Some people say she was the largest leopardess that they had ever seen. In any case, Paradise's mother was about a third heavier again than her daughter would grow up to be. But where Paradise got her nonchalant attitude with respect to almost everything (including lions) from, or her complete indifference to cars and tourists, is a mystery. To take one example, Paradise sat on the edge of Fig-Tree Avenue while a lion crept up on her from behind. Paradise paid the lion absolutely no attention. As the lion sprang at her, she just hopped to the side, and the lion landed next to her. This is almost unbelievable behaviour on the part of a leopard in the face of a deadly enemy. Paradise was also the only leopard that I have ever seen who used cars as camouflage when she crept up on prey, and who even crept under cars as she approached her quarry. If Paradise wanted to get from A to B, for example, and if 5 or 8 cars stood in the way, full of tourists wanting to look at her, then she would never take the most direct route, but would always zig-zag from car to car, always using the vehicles as cover.

PARADISE BECOMES HALF-TAIL

Paradise had adapted to her new home and had settled down. She was one of around 250 leopards in the Masai Mara, a territory in south-western Kenya of around 5000 km2, of which around 1,500 km2 forms the game reserve. The reserve borders on the northern Serengeti and, with the Serengeti, forms one of the last large and intact ecosystems in the world. In one of the most beautiful parts of the Masai Mara, between the Aitong mountains and the Mara river, lies a somewhat rocky area where Leopard Canyon and Fig-Tree Avenue are to be found.

What for us humans Alaksa or Hawaii are as holiday destinations, so must this place be as a home for leopards – that is, a dream come true. Paradise came to call this place home, but made a big mistake in the Summer of 1992. Up until then she had kept herself to herself, apart from her openness towards visitors, which they loved. But her nonchalance and lack of concern led her to attack a large herd of baboons one fine day, on a rocky plateau almost exactly half way between Fig-Tree Avenue and Leopard Canyon. During the attack she caught and killed one of the baboons' young. This enraged the male baboons in the group to such an extent that they all jumped upon Paradise in their anger, and in a joint action bit off a part of her long, beautiful tail. For a while, all you could see was a ball of leopard spots and five or six large male baboons thrashing around on the ground in a big cloud of dust. Paradise finally managed to break free and fled into a high tree – but with only half of her tail left. From then on she was impossible to mistake for any other leopard, and her name was changed to Half-Tail.

BEAUTY – HER FIRST DAUGHTER

In November 1992, Half-Tail gave birth to her first surviving cub. It was a female, and because she looked so fantastic with her full-length tail when she stood next to her mother with her short one – we christened the little one "Beauty".

Perhaps Half-Tail had already given birth to cubs before. The signs had been there, such as swollen teats, bleeding and so forth. But it often happens in the wild that the first litter of cubs which a leopardess gives birth to does not survive. In the current litter too, from which only Beauty survived into adulthood, there was probably a second cub who did not survive the first few days.

Half-Tail had brought her daughter Beauty into the world in a rocky cave near Fig-Tree Avenue. For the first few weeks she remained with her in this region, until she eventually moved with the cub to an area around 5 km away at the beginning of January. The region is called Emarti ya Faru, which roughly translated means "Land of the Rhinos". Unfortunately there are no longer any rhinos there, however, as they have all been poached for reasons which are well known.

Left: Her son Mang'aa aged around 2 months.

The two leopards lived there for the next three months, and Half-Tail taught her daughter everything that a young leopard needs to know: which animals are enemies, which are harmless, with which animals a truce is in force, as long as there is no food at stake (e.g. hyenas), and so forth. In April, both of them suddenly disappeared. Occasionally you might see them here and there, and it was clear that Half-Tail was now showing her daughter around the whole territory of around 30-40 km2.

In September 1993, that is, when she was only ten months old, Beauty began to become independent – which is quite astonishing, because according to the literature young leopards only start to break away from their mother when they are 18 months old.

In South Africa, research has shown that the young leopards there were unable to kill larger animals such as impalas or Thompson gazelles by themselves, even at 22 months of age. Their mothers always did it for them. Yet Beauty managed it when she was just 12 months old! A quite astonishing little girl.

MANG'AA UND TARATIBU

In November 1993 we discovered why Beauty had become independent at such an improbably early age. Half-Tail had had two new babies, which she also gave birth to on Fig-Tree Avenue. She chose a rocky cave, which was only 200m away from the cave where she had given birth to Beauty, her first daughter. This time she had a daughter and a son. Later, when we got to know the two leopard cubs better, we named them Taratibu and Mang'aa, which in the local language means something akin to "Prudent" and "Carefree".

The daughter Taratibu really was cautious, always staying behind Mummy, or always in a safe hiding place when she wasn't there. By contrast, the son Mang'aa had obviously inherited his mother's cool and relaxed attitude. He would lie quite openly for hours on large boulders, where everyone could see him; or he would stalk Elephants when he was only four months old, coming as close as three metres to them, while Taratibu watched her brother's antics from a safe distance.

Beauty, the older sister, did not break off contact with her mother and her young siblings however. She still lived in her mother's home territory, and sometimes caught animals very close to the cave where her brother and sister lay, leaving them in trees very close by.

Sometimes, Half-Tail would even let Beauty play with her young siblings – behaviour which has probably never before been captured in a photograph.

Previous double page: Left – two pictures of Half-Tail, the mother. Right – two pictures of Beauty, her daughter, aged around 18 months

Left: Mother Half-Tail has inspected a cave, but has not taken the cubs there. They were in another cave around 1-2 km away.

In November 1994, when she was almost exactly a year old, the cautious Taratibu was killed by a lioness during the night. We found her dead early one morning on open land, and could tell from the bite marks and the paw-prints in the mud that it must have been a lioness which had killed her. Soon afterwards, we also discovered the lioness, which showed unmistakable signs of having been in a fight: fresh scratch marks to her upper body, along with a closed and heavily swollen eye with a bleeding scratch wound, which Taratibu must have given her as she fought desperately for her life. Lions are the leopards' deadly enemies, and lions never miss the opportunity of killing a leopard.

Below: Mother Half-Tail drinking.

ZAWADI – THE SECOND ONLY-CUB

At the end of January 1996, Half-Tail had two more cubs, which she gave birth to this time in Leopard Canyon. One of the two little ones died very soon after, though. I last saw it when it was around four weeks old. Whether it was lions, hyenas, illness or some other cause which killed it, I don't know. The surviving cub was a very darkly coloured female and – like her mother – not in the least bit shy. The little leopardess seemed to take after her mother in terms of character, just like Mang'aa, who at aged about two-and-a-half years is still completely carefree when it comes to cars. Beauty on the other hand has become much more shy and always disappears immediately whenever cars come

near her. Only when she is together with her mother, which still happens sometimes, does she forget her shyness of cars.

It is interesting that the home territories of Half-Tail (the mother) and Beauty (the daughter) still overlap, even though the daughter is now already three-and-a-half years old. In March 1996 I saw the two leopards together once again. The daughter Beauty had killed a young warthog and left it in a tree, about two kilometres from the mother's third litter of cubs. Later I saw the mother and the older daughter happily feasting together on their prey.

The younger son Mang'aa, at two-and-a-half years old, still lives within his mother's territory – and in the desirable south-western quarter to boot, in the area around the "no camping" forest.

Half-Tail devoted much more attention to this daughter as an only cub than she did to the litter before. We have never seen a female leopard be so attentive to her cubs as she is with this daughter. The mother was together with her much more often during the day that she had been with previous cubs, and she played and frolicked with her much longer and more intensively than she ever did with her previous cubs. She seemed to nurture a particularly close and affectionate relationship with this one.

As we had named the first daughter Beauty three years ago, and the daughter from the second litter Taratibu (prudent) and the son Mang'aa (carefree) two-and-a-half years ago, we now gave this daughter the name Zawadi (gift), because her behaviour had brought us such magical sights.

Above: Half-Tail has discovered a hyena.

Above: Here, the daughter Taratibu at aged 10 weeks walks with her mother to a new hiding place. While the son Mang'aa was quite carefree, and sometimes even reckless, the daughter Taratibu was always frightened and "over-cautious". She never ran ahead, but always remained beside her mother or close behind her, and waited to see what her brother did first. She would only follow him across a clearing once he had already successfully and safely crossed it.

Left: Tragically, her cautious nature did nothing to help her in the end: One night, when she was 12 months old, she was killed by a lion when she was walking with her mother and brother across a wide area of open ground.

Above: A picture of Taratibu at three months old, with a somewhat sceptical look!

Overleaf: Mang'aa, the brother, had killed his first large animal at the age of one. It was a Thompson gazelle, and he carried it into this tree. He was so excited about his first successful hunt, which happened one morning at 7 o'clock, that he did not leave the tree until late in the evening.

A MAASAI ARROW

In December 1996, Half-Tail had a nasty experience. A young Maasai about 20-years old seriously wounded her with an arrow, which was left sticking in her head. The park ranger flew a vet in from Nairobi, who drugged her with a dart gun and removed the arrow. The ranger shot a Thompson gazelle and left it on the ground near the sedated leopard, so that she would have food for the first day when she awoke from the sedation. Half-Tail was lucky: the wound healed without complications, and after a few weeks there was nothing left to be seen of the injury. The young Maasai was later expelled from his village on account of this malicious act.

DEATH AMONG THE ROCKS

In October 1997, Half-Tail again gave birth to two cubs – in Leopard Canyon, just like the last ones. Unfortunately, these cubs were not to be granted a long and happy leopard life. A few weeks later an unknown leopard male about three years old (not the father of the cubs) came prowling through the territory, and discovered the two little ones, a few weeks old, in their cave. He killed them while their mother was away. When Half-Tail came back a little while later, and discovered the leopard, a wild fight ensued, during which the male leopard fell about six metres out of a tree and then disappeared. We know that male lions kill the cubs of females they do not know when they take over a pride of female lions. I had never observed this before in leopards – probably because these particular big cats lead such secretive lives.

WASIWASI AND SHUJAA

In early October 1998, at about seven o'clock in the morning in the area around the Kichwa-Tembo bush, I met Half-Tail with a young warthog in her jaws, striding purposefully and in a straight line across the Savannah. After about half an hour of walking, she reached a deep ditch, disappeared into it, and appeared again on the other side. Immediately a little leopard around three months old came running towards her, greeting its mother excitedly. It played with her and then drank milk from her. A good half an hour later a second little leopard appeared, very shy and very cautious. It did not drink milk from its mother outside in the open as its sister had done, the mother had to go with him into the safety of the bushes before he would drink.

Later, we christened this male leopard cub Wasiwasi, which means "shy". His sister, who in the following weeks proved herself to be brave and carefree, we named Shujaa, which means strong and decisive.

Half-Tail had given birth to her first two litters on Fig-Tree Avenue. The following two were born in Leopard Canyon not far away. The fact that she did not give birth to these two new cubs in the same place, but around 6-8 km away between Kichwa Tembo bush and the Mara River, may have something to do with the fact that her last two cubs were killed by a male leopard in the area of Leopard Canyon. Since this traumatic event, Half-Tail often avoids her traditional core territory, and now spends more time in this new area, which the Maasai call "Mataneti".

It seems to be an ideal area for a leopard with two small cubs: In the last two weeks we have seen no male leopards, no hyenas and no Maasai – in other words it is paradise.

Half-Tail's first daughter probably gave birth to her first cubs in 1997, but these were presumably killed by the same male leopard. In March 1999 her daughter Zawadi had her first two cubs, and Half-Tail became a grandmother. In Summer 1999, the leopardess known as Half-Tail would have been twelve years old. Unfortunately she was killed in July of that year by a Maasai herdsman's spear, as he tried to protect his herd of goats from an attack by the leopardess.

It marked the end of an era in the Masai Mara.

Mother Half-Tail with her last cubs: Wasiwasi (below) and Shujaa in the picture on the opposite page.

Above: Mother Half-Tail with her first daughter Beauty, who came into the world in November 1992.

Right: Daughter Zawadi (she was renamed "Shadow" for the television series "Great Big Cat Diary") in November 2002 with an impala which she had just caught and killed. Born at the end of January 1996, she was already nearly 7 years old in November 2002.

NEWS FROM THE FAMILY...

Zawadi, Half-Tail's third daughter, had given birth to three cubs in August, and this was what brought me to the Masai Mara at the start of November 2002. I wanted to photograph mother and cub together; and you have the best chance of doing this when the little ones are three months old. Unfortunately, by the time I arrived all three of them were dead. First of all, two of them had been killed by hyenas, and one week later the last remaining cub vanished too. As the Maasai had been burning a large portion of Zawadi's home range (as our own farmers are often wont to do with their land), we can only assume that the last cub met its end amid the flames.

Over the last year, all three of Zawadi's cubs were killed by Hyenas, and in the previous year an unknown male leopard had killed two of Zawadi's cubs from that year. Only a single daughter, which we named "Dark", and who is now three years old, has so far survived out of all of Zawadi's offspring. If only one cub survives out of a total of nine over three years, then that is an indication of some pretty tough living conditions indeed.

After Half-Tail's daughter Taratibu had been killed by a lioness in December 1994, we had named the next daughter Zawadi, which translates as "gift". I have known Zawadi since her first months of life, that is, for about 6 years. At that time I had been searching for mother Half-Tail and the three-month-old Zawadi for more than a week in their home range in the Masai Mara in Kenya before I eventually found them, just before nightfall, close to Leopard Canyon. Half-Tail was lying in the grass relaxing and her daughter was drinking mother's milk from her. Then she began to run around somewhat as a hyena suddenly appeared. This helped me to take one of my most beautiful pictures of this little leopardess.

When the little Zawadi saw the hyenas coming, she ran straight to a tree and leaned against it, so that she could climb up it any time she wanted. At the same time, she looked from her mother to the hyena and back to her mother, to see if the hyena would come any closer and to see if her mother would give her an instruction as to what she should do. But the hyena continued on its way. The tense situation abated, and I had taken a wonderful picture in the last rays of the sun. I used a 4.0/600 mm lens, 1/30 seconds, with an open shutter and with ISO 400 Provia film, as there was insufficient light to justify using a better film.

In November 2002 I met Zawadi, who was by now over 6 years old, just once close to Kichwa Temba bush, as she was catching a young impala and carrying it safely into a tree away from lions and hyenas. Take a look at the picture on the opposite page.

Leopard-watching by Night

BETWEEN DAY-TIME AND DREAM-TIME IN THE SECRET WORLD OF LEOPARDS

It was nearly 5 pm. In a tree in front of me in Kenya's Masai Mara game reserve there hung a dead impala – still completely uneaten but definitely dead. Under the tree lay Half-Tail, the mother leopard. Next to her a few metres away lay her two youngest cubs, Mang'aa and Taratibu, both around half a year old, and about 15 m away the older daughter, Beauty, who was a year older than her two siblings. All four of them were almost invisible in the long grass.

The mother was probably guarding the prey for the two cubs, because whenever the older daughter came close to the tree with the food in it, Half-Tail would growl menacingly at her.

This was how the situation remained until I had to leave the area when night fell, because you are not allowed to stay overnight in the reserve except in the camps. Very early the next morning I was able to take the following picture: not a single leopard left to be seen, and the fully-grown impala completely devoured – only the skull and horns lying under the tree as sole evidence of the previous night's feasting.

Left: The leopardess had left a topi under this tree in the morning and had not paid it any more attention for the rest of the day. Not until the following night did she return, carrying the animal into the safety of a high tree.

79

Had the mother eaten first, or the older daughter? Or first the two cubs and then the mother? Or the mother together with the two little ones and then the older daughter? Or perhaps all four leopards devoured the impala together, either in or under the tree?

I would have loved to have seen it myself with my camera and flashlight. I promised myself then and there that the next chance I got I would take photographs of leopards at night.

That is easier said than done, however! First you have to have leopards who can regularly and reliably be found at a certain place. The best time for this is when a leopardess has cubs who are around 3-4 months old. As long as the cubs are younger than this, they will live hidden in caves, ditches and bushes, and when they are older and bigger they will often move around with their mother so that the cubs can get to know their home and the dangers of life as a leopard. You waste a great deal of time looking for them every day!

But when leopards are three or four months old they are already very active, climbing into trees and over rocks even when their mother isn't there. And their mother comes by almost every day, or every night, so that the cubs can have their milk. At least, that's the theory. We wildlife photographers may want things that way, but the leopards may have other ideas!

Around two years after the event I described at the start of this chapter, we had come this far: Half-Tail had given birth to two new cubs on 28th January, and in mid-April I was there to photograph the mother with her third litter of young kittens – but this time by night, at least that was the plan.

Above: A scene which until recently was thought to be impossible: The mother lies in front of the cave and watches over her two small cubs while the older, one-year-old daughter lies close by watching them, and playing with her younger siblings.

One of the two leopard cubs was unfortunately killed before I arrived. He was last seen at the end of February aged about four weeks. Whether lions, hyenas, illness or other causes led to his death, I can't say. The surviving cub was a very darkly coloured female and, like its mother, not in the least bit shy. When I saw her for the first time, just before sunset on 17th April, she was looking inquisitively over a rocky ledge towards my car. Then she climbed into a very leafy tree, because a hyena suddenly strolled by, and stayed there until it got quite dark. We waited a while longer, but Half-Tail was nowhere to be seen.

The little leopardess seemed to take after her mother in terms of character, just like Mang'aa, who at about two-and-a-half years old is still completely carefree when it comes to cars. Beauty on the other hand has become much more shy and always disappears immediately whenever cars come near her. Only when she is together with her mother, which still happens sometimes, does she forget her shyness of cars. It is interesting that the home territories of Half-Tail, the mother, and Beauty, the daughter, still overlap, even though the daughter is now already three-and-a-half years old. In March 1996 I saw the two leopards together once again. The daughter Beauty had killed a young warthog and left it in a tree, about two kilometres from the mother's third litter of cubs. Later I saw the mother and the older daughter happily feasting together on their prey. The younger son Mang'aa, at two-and-a-half years old, still lives in his mother's territory – and in the desirable south-western quarter to boot, in the area around the "no camping" forest.

For the planned night-time leopard hunt, armed with a camera, I had to make a great deal of preparations. Firstly, I had to obtain the relevant permit to allow me to drive around at night time at all. Then an infrared lamp, which gets its power from the car's cigarette lighter, and in whose red light beam I could focus using autofocus (AF), and which would not disturb the leopards. I had already tried this out on my travels. Then a night-vision device, which would greatly amplify the available residual light, and without which you would not be able to see a single thing in the darkness. In addition, an interesting accessory from Nikon, the SK-6 power bracket which reduces the minimum cycle time between flashes from around 7 seconds down to about 3. If you are standing in the dark in front of a leopard who has just killed a zebra, and if you then have to wait seven seconds before you can take the next picture, then this will soon be enough to give you a heart attack, or pave the way for a stomach ulcer. Next came the Lepp teleflash extender. Test photographs taken in Germany at night had shown that the SB-24 – with a reflector setting of 85 mm – with the Sensia

100 with shutter 2.8 was sufficient for distances of up to 10 m. With the Lepp extender you could easily go to 25 m. In practice, this meant that for distances of up to 25 m I uses the Sensia 100 [erroneously "Sensia-1 00" in original], and if the leopards or other animals were further away I used the Sensia 400. Test photos had been taken, the relevant permit was in place – the infrared searchlight, night-vision equipment, teleflash extender and flash-cycle reducer were all ready for action, the little leopard had been found: everything was ready to go.

18th April: This morning we were surprised to run into the cheetah called "Queen" with her two 16-month-old cubs. She is the only female cheetah here in the Masai Mara to have developed the habit of regularly jumping onto the bonnets of cars, presumably because she knows that from there you get a very good overview of the surrounding neighbourhood and can keep a good look out for potential prey. She's not content to just stay on the bonnets for a short time though, but will often stay there for 15-30 minutes. This morning she first sat for a while on a Toyota Landcruiser from Mara Buffalo Camp, before turning her attentions to a little Suzuki belonging to a Japanese television team – who were incidentally unable to film this nice little picture.

The rest of the day was quiet, and at 5.00 pm we were in our car in Leopard Canyon, around 20m from the rocky precipice where the little leopard must actually have spent the day hidden in a cave behind some bushes.

Above: Mother Half-Tail and her two cubs Taratibu and Mang'aa resting on a termite mound as darkness falls. During the day you see this very seldom, but under cover of darkness they do not feel that they are being watched any more.

Opposite page: Half-Tail takes a stroll through Leopard Canyon with her daughter Zawadi under cover of the night.

At around 6.00 pm, in the last rays of the sun, it came out of the cave to play-hunt red-headed agama lizards on the boulders. At around 6.30 pm it suddenly disappeared, at lightning speed, back into its hiding place. From around 100 m away a rock hyrax had sounded a call, and this was warning enough to make the little leopard immediately seek the safety of the cave. What it could not know was that the warning cry of the hyrax was enough to call its mother back from her day-time resting place, a group of rocks around 2 km away, to check up on her little daughter. Unfortunately, the reunion took place away from view behind the bushes, but about ten minutes later, as it was getting dark, Half-Tail came down the rocky wall with her daughter, and lay down exactly 10 m away from our car on the grassy floor of Leopard Canyon.

The little leopardess immediately began to play with her mother, and to run up and down the rocky walls in a circuit of about 20-40 m, occasionally pausing to jump playfully onto her mother. You could see in the little leopard's movements how much she enjoyed being able to frolic around, now that her mother was here to protect her.

After about half an hour's playtime, the mother leopard slowly climbed the opposite rock wall with her cub, and disappeared with her a few minutes later into the night. Unfortunately, we could not follow the two of them over this kind of terrain, and I wished that in such situations I could swap my car for a silent helicopter.

The first evening was a complete success: All of the equipment worked perfectly, and

the leopards were not disturbed either by the infra-red light nor by the flash. I also made another wonderful discovery: As the leopardess was lying about 10 m away from the vehicle, I took photographs with the 2.8/300 mm lens with the Lepp teleflash extender in front of the Nikon SB-24 flash. With the help of the flash cycle-time reducer I seemed to have enough power at my disposal to bring the flash cycle time down to under one second. This meant that I could take photographs practically one after the other, without having to wait for the flash to re-charge.

19th April: After the leopardess had sheltered her daughter for about four weeks in two different locations in Leopard Canyon, she had now moved on without leaving a "forwarding address", and we spent the whole day searching in all of the likely areas without finding a single trace of her.

22nd April: This afternoon at about 5.00 pm we met five giraffes. One of them had their gaze fixed worriedly on a point about 100 m away in the long grass. We systematically searched the surrounding area, and finally found a dead impala buck under a fever acacia, whose right back leg had already been eaten. Perhaps the giraffe had seen the leopard creep away from its prey. When we returned again shortly before dark, the leopard was indeed eating its prey, but did not let us come any closer than about

Above: Up in a tree, two small leopards are eating a hare while their mother keeps watch below by the tree trunk.

40 m. In any case it was not our own mother Half-Tail, but a leopard who was unknown to us. Later, in the darkness, we suddenly caught site of a caracal, but unfortunately it was terribly photo-shy and immediately disappeared into the darkness.

23rd April: This afternoon we found a large group of lions with two males, three females and 14 cubs of various ages. They were all lying in or under thick bushes, to protect them from the heat. One hour before sunset they came out and began to play, but only when it got dark did they really start to move, and come out into the open savannah. Here, the cubs tried to drink from their mothers, which the mothers didn't seem too pleased about. Over and over again they bared their teeth at their cubs, or went a few metres further away to escape from the little imps. The darkness didn't help them at all – the cubs always knew exactly where their mothers were. They could obviously see in the dark just as well as they could.

24th April: This morning at about 7.00 am we finally found Half-Tail again. She was dragging a fully grown impala buck across the savannah, and you could tell from the trail it had left that she had been carrying it for at least 200 m. Finally she carried it under a thicket and lay down, completely exhausted, under a nearby tree. For five days we had seen nothing of her at all, although we had been looking for her. Now we would stay near her the whole day long, in the hope that in the evening she would lead us to her daughter.

It is remarkable that the tourists in their cars nearby could talk loudly to one another 20 m away without the leopard reacting. But when Maasai passed within 200 m, talking with one another, then she immediately became alert, ready to flee. Tourists, and primarily journalists on sponsored trips through the reserves of east Africa, sometimes imagine that the animals will be very disturbed by five or ten vehicles, whose passengers look, take photographs and talk loudly nearby. It is not always clear to them that these convoys only stop for a short while near a particular animal before moving on.

So it was today: Between 9.00 and 10.00 am, a number of tourist vehicles came by, and then again on the afternoon run at about 5.00 pm. In the 13 hours that I was there, no other vehicle was to be seen for at least 11 hours, and the leopardess slept, rested or dozed the whole day long in the shadow of trees near her prey, changing position every one or two hours, and twice eating at the dead animal.

In fact, nothing happened for the whole day, until she once again went to her prey and ate at it for ten minutes as twilight descended. In the mean time half of the impala had gone and I actually expected her to carry the remainder into a tree, but nothing happened. When it then became really dark, she wandered leisurely down to a waterhole about 80 m away, and drank thirstily. Two or three minutes later you could suddenly hear hyenas fighting over the dead impala. Presumably they had been in the area for a long time and had just been waiting for the right moment when we – the leopard and the car – moved away from the prey.

The leopard heard them too of course, and went cautiously half way back to the dead animal, stood still for a moment, as if considering what to do next, and then wandered slowly off into the night. She knew, of course, that she had no chance whatsoever of getting her prey back off a group of between three and five hyenas.

Above: This six month old male leopard loves to sleep on termite mounds, while his anxious sister always searches out a less comfortable, but safer tree for the night time.

The hyenas attacking the food were making quite scary noises, which I had never heard during daylight before, and it sounded as if a serious and dogged fight was going on over the spoils of the dead impala buck. I would have loved to have seen that with the night-vision equipment and photographed it with my camera and flash, but I now had a decision to make: either to photograph hyenas up to their tricks or to follow the leopard into the dark night, so as to perhaps discover the little daughter's new cave. I decided in favour of the leopard, and we followed it for about one and a half hours. But then it entered an area full of large stones, where we had absolutely no chance of following by the car, and so we completely lost the trail.

Night-vision goggles (low-light amplifiers) are amazing: put simply, you can see absolutely nothing with the naked eye, but with night-vision equipment you can see everything. So during the time we were able to follow the leopardess, there were two interesting encounters: firstly, a pigeon suddenly landed in front of her on the beaten track which the leopard had been using for a long time. The pigeon let the leopard come to within about 2-3 m of her. When she then flew away, the leopard jumped up and tried to bat her with her claws, just like a pet cat tries to bat a ball of wool thrown towards it.

The second encounter during the night was even more interesting: suddenly the leopard stood still. She had discovered a hyena 50 m away, and then ran quickly into a tree about 20 m away. The hyena followed her and I thought that the leopard would now jump into the tree. Instead, she just sat under it, and when the hyena was close to her, the leopard lay on her side. I had already observed this behaviour twice before during daylight in previous years, that this leopard lay on her side whenever hyenas or male baboons came close to her. The Hyena circled the leopard once, and then moved on. The leopard waited a moment, and then also continued on her way. Why on earth did she run under the tree, if she did not then want to climb it? Perhaps this was just an insurance policy, in case the hyena decided to attack, or in case other hyenas followed. Perhaps, on the other hand, she had not been able to tell immediately that it was a hyena, and not a lion! After all, it was pitch dark, and only we with our night-vision equipment could see everything completely clearly.

25th April: Today, too, we searched from 6.00 am in the morning for the mother and her daughter, unfortunately with no success. But at 6.10 pm – it was only 20 minutes before twilight descended – we suddenly saw the daughter, two metres up in a fever acacia tree. Then we discovered mother Half-Tail too, who was lying a few meters away in the long grass, and 10 m further away stood a hyena, who probably wanted to see whether their was any food to be had from the leopards. In the end it was her we had to thank for the fact that we had discovered the little leopard at all, because she had probably fled into the tree because of the hyena. Without the hyena, she would have certainly been lying in the grass next to her mother. After the hyena had finally moved on, the little cub climbed down from the tree, ran to its mother and began to drink milk from her. After nightfall, both of them made their way to Leopard Canyon around 500 m away, which they sized up along its entire length before finally climbing up a rock wall at the far end and disappearing.

26th April: This morning we were of course already up just it was getting light, and soon found the young female leopard cub climbing around the place. At about 7.00 am mother Half-Tail also appeared, and climbed into a lone tree which stood on the upper edge of Leopard Canyon. She soon came down again with a fully-grown male grivet monkey in her jaws. She must have caught it during the night and left it up in the tree. Both of the leopards began to eat it. After about half an hour, the little leopard cub who was by now almost exactly three months old, took the adult monkey and dragged it to a tree about 10 m away, which it wanted to climb along with his prey. Three times it tried, and three times it fell out of the tree from about half a metre up, with the monkey, landing on its back in the grass with the monkey on top of it. It was a picture fit for a king. After five minutes the mother leopard came and took the dead monkey off the daughter, taking her back to the place where they were before. Then they both ate the monkey together until there was nothing left.

As we had named the first daughter Beauty three years ago, and two-and-a-half years ago named the daughter from the second litter Taratibu (prudent) and the son Mang'aa (carefree), we now gave this daughter the name Zawadi (gift), because through her behaviour she had given us such magical sights.

Night time in the African bush is a relatively unexplored area, both scientifically and photographically, and there is still much work to be done in this area. A lot happens in one night in Africa's wilderness that goes un-photographed and unobserved…

Man and Leopards

Roughly 25 million years ago there were many different species of big cat, of which only seven survive in our present age. Fossils provide evidence of the development of the lives of these cats on our planet. Big cat species such as the leopard were up until relatively recently regarded simply as bestial brutes, and accounts and diaries of hunters from the last two hundred years, which now seem rather comical to us, were intended to be taken entirely seriously at the time they were written.

Here is a short extract from a hunter's diary which was still being published in 1989:

"I was standing in the open skylight of a VW camper van... when I saw a striking dark spot about 100 m away, like the shadow of an outline, in the gently swaying, sand-coloured grass of the savannah. There was no doubt that it was a leopard, ducking and diving around! ... Slowly we drew close to the animal as it crouched in front of us. Then it suddenly raised its rounded head and stared at us as if spellbound, without making a sound as you might expect a lion to do. Standing in the open sliding roof of the

Previous page: A leopard lies completely relaxed on a rock under a fig tree, almost directly in the centre of the picture. The many humans and cars around do not disturb it in the least. It is an ideal relationship between cat and man. Wouldn't it be nice if it could always be like this.

Opposite page: If you look closely you will see a leopard carefully watching the Maasai walking towards their village.

Above: A leopard is watching the shepherds and their animals. The leopards know the Maasai, and know from long experience that it is advisable to keep away from them and their herds.

van, from my vantage point I expected to see the wild animal jump and run away, but what actually happened was something quite different. When we were just 10 m away from the big cat, in a flash it began to attack our vehicle as we drew closer. With a long, hoarse, gurgling and snarling noise, and with its fangs bared in anger, the mighty leopard stormed at us three or four times, growling angrily. As I dropped into the safety of the van in terror, the animal which we had disturbed took a terrific leap about 1-2 m in front of the windscreen, then spun away at the last moment, just before impact, diving into the thick grass. What a to-do! We were petrified."

The poor hunter, and how dangerous their lives must have been! How easy it would have been for the leopard to climb through the open roof and drag the hunter out, carrying him off to its four cubs for breakfast! Perish the thought. But it all turned out well in the end, as, in fact, did all of the old hunting stories. At the last minute, luck or the hunter's presence of mind always saves him from the wrath of the terrifying beast.

That leopards are thinking and feeling beings, that mother leopards treat and bring up their cubs in much the same way that we do, never entered people's heads before. Historically, the bonds between leopard and man were always purely economic. Humans wanted leopards for their pelts or were (and are) concerned lest leopards attack their cattle or pets.

The relationship between an individual human and leopards depends to a large extent on their own personal interest. Women may want to wear a dead one as clothing; the hunter wants to catch it and kill

Top: Young leopards love to play under cars and to smell the tyres, before climbing over them.

Middle: When a leopard hunts, it uses every available cover, including cars. Nothing is out of bounds, not even a Toyota.

92

it, the farmer, peasant or Maasai would gladly send them all to hell, the tourist wants to watch them, the nature lover loves them.

Leopards are highly intelligent and can recognise and take account of changes in their environment very quickly, and adapt to them accordingly.

As long as hunting was allowed in Kenya, in the 19th century, there would have been virtually zero chance of being able to observe a leopard in the flesh. The leopards were extremely shy, and practically never showed themselves during daylight hours. Furthermore, they avoided all contact with humans. Today, you can come across leopards practically any time in the right places, during broad daylight. They no longer run away even from Maasai, but rather they just duck out of sight or walk nonchalantly past, even quite close by.

In the mean time, the leopards of the Masai Mara seem to have incorporated the vehicles from the camps and lodges into their 'biotope'. For example, if a group of around five vehicles are crossing a wide open space – which leopards do not like to cross during the day – then the leopards will not simply cross the open space, but will go from vehicle to vehicle, always using them as cover.

And I have also seen it happen several times, that a leopard on one side of a Land Rover will creep up on its intended prey the

other side of the vehicle, and then crawl under it to emerge on the other side, and so use the vehicle with 4-6 tourists on board as cover for a surprise attack.

Top: A leopard is always an attraction for tourists, and a highlight of the day. The vehicles stop longer for leopards than for any other animal.

Middle: Seldom captured on camera: Here the leopard is watching its prey on the other side of the vehicle. Later, it crawled under the vehicle and made a surprise attack. Cats learn quickly, and if we don't hunt them, kill them, or destroy their habitat, then we can have a share in their fascinating lives.

Where to Stay to see Leopards

KENYA

Masai Mara National Reserve
Samburu National Reserve
Lake Nakuru National Park

TANZANIA

Serengeti National Park
Ngorongoro Crater Reserve

SOUTH AFRICA

There are a large number of small reserves around the Krüger National Park which are excellent for leopard-watching, such as the Sabi Sands Game Reserve, which includes Mala Mala and the famous leopard region of Londolozi.

WEBSITES

You can find detailed information on parks and big cats at the following web addresses:

http://www.newafrica.com/nationalparks/

http://www.africat.org

dialspace.dial.pipex.com/agarman/bco/ver4.htm

www.bigcats.com

Above: One of the best and most beautiful places in the northern Masai Mara is Leopard Canyon. Over ten thousand visitors must have watched leopards here – alone or with their cubs.

94

Photo Hints and Tips

If all you want to do is to see leopards and take snaps, then of course you can just join one of the regular tourist groups which visit the national parks and nature reserves of Africa, and you will probably be lucky enough to capture a leopard on film.

But if you want to take really good leopard shots, then you'll probably want to join a proper photography tour. Such tours exist to enable people to take really good pictures of Africa's animals including their big cats. Examples of such tours include those run by Joseph Van Os Photo Safaris (www.photosafaris.com) or Joe McDonald (www.hoothollow.com).

But the very best way to get the best possible leopard pictures is, unfortunately, also the most expensive and the most time-consuming; namely to travel on your own (or with a driver), to search for the leopards yourself and then, when you find them, to stay close to them from sunrise to sunset. That way you will have the very best chance of seeing something truly photogenic, which you can then capture on film.

For this, you will need a 100-400 mm zoom lens and, if possible, an additional 500 or 600 mm fixed focus lens. If the leopard is in a tree, then the best thing to do is to take photographs from your vehicle's skylight with a sandbag as a camera rest. If the leopard is on the ground then a side window is best, because this gives better perspective. You can get special camera stands for car windows from your dealer, which are better suited to the task than sand bags. They have certain advantages if you're looking to take snapshots. But the three things you need most when photographing leopards are patience, patience, and more patience.

All photographs in this book are authentic documents. They have not been doctored or digitally manipulated in any way.

BIBLIOGRAPHY

Estes, R.D: *The Behavior Guide to African Mammals*,
University of California Press Berkeley 1991

Hagen, W; Hagen, H; Pölking, F: *Der Leopard*,
Tecklenborg Verlag Steinfurt 1995

Leyhausen, Paul: *Katzen, eine Verhaltenskunde*,
Verlag Paul Parey Berlin & Hamburg 1960/1982

Pölking, F: *Leoparden*, Tecklenborg Verlag, Steinfurt 1995

Pölking, F: *Fotoprojekt Masai Mara*, GDT Lünen 1995

Scott, J: *The Leopard's Tale*, ELM Tree Books London 1985

Scott, J. & A: *Mara-Serengeti A Photographer's Paradise*,
Fountain Press Faringdon Oxon 2000

Scott, J. & A: *Big Cat Diary Leopard*, HarperCollins
London 2003

This young, but already independent leopard had fled into the cave to escape from three hyenas. After half and hour he came to the entrance and looked cautiously out to see whether the hyenas were still there or not.